# BUS OPERATORS 1970
# North West England and Yorkshire

## Gavin Booth

Ian Allan
PUBLISHING

# Contents

Front cover: In the early days of Merseyside PTE, a former Liverpool Corporation 1957 Leyland Titan PD2/20 with Crossley 62-seat body, at Brownlow Hill, Liverpool, in June 1970.
Mark Page

Back cover, upper: Standard BET Group fare for Yorkshire Woollen, a 1965 Leyland Leopard PSU3/4R with Weymann 53-seat body, at Wakefield in May 1970 alongside a former Bristol Omnibus Bristol FLF Lodekka drafted in to the newly state-owned West Riding fleet.
Mark Page

Back cover, lower: Representing the Doncaster area independents, still an important local force in 1970, is this Felix, Hatfield, 1962 AEC Regent V 2D3RA with 73-seat Roe body, at Thorne. Felix would be the first of the Doncaster independents to sell out to South Yorkshire PTE in the 1970s.
Mark Page

Previous page: Leyland chassis and East Lancs bodies cropped up regularly in north-west England and Yorkshire, particularly in municipal fleets. This late-model Titan PD3/14 with 70-seat forward entrance body, seen in the centre of Stockport, was delivered new to Stockport Corporation in 1969, but was photographed after it had been absorbed into the new Selnec PTE fleet, hence the four-figure fleetnumber and the side advertising.
Ted Jones

This page: Leeds bought single-deckers for driver-only operation in the late1960s/early 1970s including this Daimler Fleetline SRG6LXB with 48-seat Park Royal body, one of 30 bought in 1970.
R Johnson

Facing page: Through the British Railways involvement, Sheffield's B and C fleets were able to buy ECW bodies on Leyland chassis. This is a 1957 Titan PD2/20 59-seater at Dewsbury in 1970 following transfer from the C fleet to the Yorkshire Woollen company following the 1970 dissolution of the Sheffield Joint Omnibus Committee.
M A Penn

First published 2007

ISBN (10) 0 7110 3202 5
ISBN (13) 978 0 7110 3202 6

© Ian Allan Publishing Ltd 2007
Design by Hieroglyph
Published by Ian Allan Publishing
An imprint of Ian Allan Publishing Ltd, Riverdene Business Park, Molesey Road, Hersham, Surrey KT12 4RGS
Printed by Ian Allan Printing Ltd, Riverdene Business Park, Molesey Road, Hersham, Surrey KT12 4RG
Code: 0706/B1

Visit the Ian Allan Publishing website at www.ianallanpublishing.com

# Introduction

This is the last in a series of five books taking a whistle-stop tour around Britain as it was in 1970. That year was chosen for good reasons as the bus industry was undergoing major changes following the 1968 Transport Act that created the National Bus Company, the Scottish Bus Group, and the first Passenger Transport Executives, all moves that would have a significant impact on the shape of the industry for the next decade or so – until thoughts turned to deregulation and privatisation in the 1980s.

Another move that affected all operators was the introduction of the Bus Grants scheme, which gave bus operators increasingly generous grants towards the purchase of new buses that were suitable for driver-only operation. This allowed the new PTEs to replace many of the non-standard vehicle types they inherited with new standard types, and encouraged further savings in a cash-strapped industry by heralding the end of conductors in many areas. It also allowed smaller operators who had traditionally bought secondhand buses from their bigger brothers to invest in new vehicles.

For enthusiasts it also marked the end of the traditional British front-engined halfcab double-decker, consigned to history because it was not suitable for driver-only operation. So the operators who clung on to halfcabs as long as they could – and there were a few in the North-West and Yorkshire – had to consider other types. Some operators had moved to single-deckers in a big way in the days before driver-only double-deckers were permitted, and some stayed with them, while others got quickly back to double-deckers.

With the creation of the Merseyside and Selnec PTEs, the north-west saw more changes than most, and there would be further major changes in 1974 with the creation of the new metropolitan counties, leading to the setting-up of new PTEs at South Yorkshire and West Yorkshire and new constituents for the Merseyside and now renamed Greater Manchester PTEs.

With former Tilling and BET group fleets, significant independents, and municipal operators with their own individual ideas of the perfect bus, there was no shortage of vehicle interest in the North-West and Yorkshire, and it would be some years before NBC corporatism or PTE standard designs swept all of this away.

I am grateful to the band of photographers who supplied colour and black-and-white photos for this and the previous books in the series. I am also grateful to the books and magazines I used for background research. I have sometimes wondered why I keep so many publications, but these books would not have happened without well-thumbed copies of *Buses Illustrated* magazine (predecessor of today's *Buses*), the British Bus Fleets series of ABC-style fleetlists, and A M Whitton's series of Fleetbooks that took over the British Bus Fleets mantle in the 1970s. The book 'Municipal Buses in Colour 1959-1974' by the late Reg Wilson was also well-used, and I also found myself referring constantly to an excellent 1982 book, 'The Ordnance Survey Atlas of Great Britain'. ∎

**Gavin Booth**
**Edinburgh**

# North-West England and Yorkshire Snapshot

Back in 1970 more than one in every five UK residents lived in the north-west and Yorkshire – over 12 million of them – and nearly eight million lived in the four great conurbations, what we know today as Greater Manchester, Merseyside, South Yorkshire and West Yorkshire. But the area covered by this book is considerably greater, taking in what was still known at the time as Cumberland, Westmorland, Lancashire, Cheshire, and the East, West and North Ridings of Yorkshire.

Four cities dominate the area – Leeds, Liverpool, Manchester and Sheffield – and the road and rail systems reflect this. These are areas that in 1970 relied on traditional industries like mechanical engineering, vehicle building, and textiles and clothing; in South Yorkshire much of the economy relied on mining. Over the next decades the deep coal mining industry disappeared and vehicle builders like Leyland, very relevant to this book, would disappear into the hands of multinational companies.

North of the conurbations, of course, there is some of England's most beautiful countryside, with areas like the Lake District, the Yorkshire Dales and the North York Moors. And coastal resorts like Blackpool, Bridlington, Morecambe, Scarborough, Southport and Whitby were still attracting coachloads of day and holiday visitors in 1970, although the growth of overseas package holidays would soon change that.

Two of the first of the new Passenger Transport Executives (PTEs) had just been set up, introducing us to the new acronym Selnec, and establishing Merseyside as a distinct region. Selnec (South-east Lancashire and North-East Cheshire) encompassed 11 former municipal undertakings and inherited some 2,500 buses; Merseyside PTE was formed from three municipals and started with some 1,000 buses.

The other new entity was the National Bus Company (NBC), which took over the state-owned Tilling and British Electric Traction (BET) group companies, and which operated some 5,000 buses and coaches in the area concerned – although this includes all of the 1,000-plus vehicles in the Chester-based Crosville fleet, already covered in the Midlands and Wales volume in this series.

The 24 remaining municipal operators, even without the 3,500 buses removed from the total, were still an important force. Between them they had 3,680 buses in 1970, though the creation of the South Yorkshire and West Yorkshire PTEs in 1974, and further boundary changes in Greater Manchester and Merseyside, would see 10 further casualties, leaving just under 1,200 buses in local authority control.

The area also included a number of significant and well-known independent operators. In bus terms, by far the largest was 396-vehicle Lancashire United Transport; following West Riding's acquisition by the state at the end of 1967 and consequent absorption into the new National Bus Company, LUT was the UK's largest independent bus company, ahead of 330-vehicle Barton Transport. Also in the north-west and Yorkshire was the country's largest coach operator, Wallace Arnold, with over 300 vehicles.

Although most other independents had relatively small fleets, typically with fewer than 30 vehicles, they included some well-known names, including a couple that survive today. The survivors are Fishwick, Leyland and Pennine, Gargrave, but casualties since 1970 include the famous Doncaster area firms, most of which sold out to the new South Yorkshire PTE.

And it was the PTEs that would strongly influence the shape of the bus industry in the north-west and Yorkshire in the shorter-term. Already Selnec and Merseyside were making their mark, and Selnec would soon absorb much of NBC's North Western company. And in South and West Yorkshire, the 1974 creation of new PTEs would affect NBC and independent operators quite significantly. ∎

The newly-created Selnec PTE sought to find a livery that had no connection with any of the constituent municipal fleets and came up with this striking orange/white scheme carried here by a former Manchester Corporation 1963 Leyland Titan PD2/37 with 65-seat Metro-Cammell Orion bodywork seen in Manchester in 1970; in the background is one of the trend-setting Mancunian double-deckers still in Manchester colours.
Tony Wilson

# Setting the scene

The north-west of England underwent greater changes to the structure of its bus services at the end of the 1960s than most other English regions when transport services in two of the UK's most significant conurbations, centred on Liverpool and Manchester, were passed into the control of the new Merseyside and Selnec PTEs. The Yorkshire conurbations, based on Leeds and Sheffield, were still served by long-standing municipal operators in 1970, but four years later the new South Yorkshire and West Yorkshire PTEs would be created.

The changes at the end of the 1960s also affected the territorial operators, when the Tilling and BET bus interests in England and Wales were brought together under the new National Bus Company at the start of 1969.

These changes resulted from the Labour Government's determination to address the steady decline in the country's transport services that was aggravated by the growth in private motoring and the spread of television, which encouraged fewer people to go out in the evenings. The 1968 Transport Act created the first four PTEs (Tyneside and West Midlands were the other two) and the framework for the new National Bus Company, a fusion of the state-owned Tilling Group and the previously separate BET Group, which was eased by BET's decision to sell its UK bus interests to the state.

There was a feeling that many bus operators were simply managing decline, and that the industry needed a shake-up to persuade it to adapt to the new challenges. One way the government tackled this was to set up a New Bus Grants scheme, which would encourage operators to buy new buses that were suitable for driver-only operation. This had the double benefit of helping operators reduce their wage bills by moving to driver-only buses in a big way, and renewing their fleets at the same time. The grant was initially 25 per cent of the cost of suitable new buses and soon rose to 50 per cent.

Needless to say, bus operators took full advantage of this generosity and the intake of new buses rose greatly. The bus grants scheme allowed new undertakings like Merseyside and Selnec PTEs to invest heavily in new standard types to replace the varied selection they had inherited from their constituent municipalities. Selnec had a particular problem, with a bewildering array of chassis and body types among the 2,500 vehicles that came from the 11 municipal fleets.

National Bus Company also set out to standardise its fleets. Tilling Group companies had highly standardised fleets, mainly products from the previously state-owned Bristol and Eastern Coach Works (ECW) stables. The BET Group had a less rigid approach to vehicle-buying, and so its companies had bought buses to suit local circumstances and indeed local preferences. The size of the BET orders meant that it tended to patronise the larger manufacturers, like AEC, Daimler and Leyland for chassis and Alexander, Metro-Cammell, Marshall and Park Royal for bodywork, but since Bristol and ECW products had come back on to the open market, these were appearing in BET fleets.

During the 1960s the UK bus manufacturing industry had been experiencing a series of mergers and takeovers, which meant that one firm, British Leyland, dominated the supply market. New buses badged as AECs, Bristols, Daimlers, Guys and Leylands were all BL products, as were bodies from ECW, Park Royal and Roe. For operators looking for substantial deliveries of full-size heavyweight buses there was little choice.

There was some choice, though. Bedford and Ford, traditionally associated with coach chassis, recognised that many bus operators with more rural operations were looking for lighter-weight, lower-price chassis, and there were other firms that were increasing their presence, well aware that there were operators who were unhappy about BL's dominance, and aware that the bus grants scheme would lead to a boom in new orders. Dennis, such a significant force in the 1990s, was not heavily involved in the bus business, but Seddon was making plans, as was MCW, which could see a threat to its bodybuilding business and was investigating links with Scania to produce complete buses.

There were more bodybuilders that were independent of BL, but they also recognised the threat to their own futures, particularly when in 1970 the prototype Leyland National integral citybus was unveiled. Firms like Marshall and Willowbrook relied heavily on single-deck body-on-chassis orders from a range of customers, and the National looked set to put that at risk. The other independent bodybuilders included names like Alexander, East Lancs, Metro-Cammell and Northern Counties, mostly involved in double-deck bodies and doubtless nervously watching what BL would do next.

The bus grants scheme effectively killed off Leyland's remaining front-engined double-deck chassis, and its main offerings were the recently-introduced Bristol VRT and the longer-running Daimler Fleetline and Leyland Atlantean. The Leyland National would soon kill off most of the single-deck rear-engined chassis, the AEC Swift, Bristol RE, Daimler Roadliner and Leyland Panther, although the trusty Leopard would soldier on for at least another decade.

The 1968 Transport Act gave the bus industry a chance to catch its breath, regroup and strengthen its position ahead of changes that nobody in 1970 could really have anticipated – the major regulatory changes of the 1980s. Looking back, if the changes around 1970 hadn't happened, the bus industry would have been in no condition to cope with the upheaval of the 1980s. ■

The Leyland Leopard, here with Willowbrook body, was a staple in fleets like Yorkshire Traction.
Mark Page

# The North-west

The area north of Manchester up to Carlisle and the Scottish border was always closely associated with the giant Ribble company, still warmly remembered by many as one of the great territorial bus companies. Although Ribble dominated a substantial part of north-west England, it was by no means the only bus operator in that area. There was the former Tilling Group company, Cumberland Motor Services; there was a group of municipal operators in a band that ran east from Blackpool and Lytham St Annes, to Preston, Blackburn, Darwen and Accrington, Rossendale and, on the edge of the Pennines, Burnley, Colne & Nelson.

Remote from these was the isolated Barrow Corporation bus operation, and the best-known independent operator in the area was, and is, Fishwick of Leyland.

Ribble's operating area covered a significant swathe of north-west England. Although the company was based in Preston, its buses could be found all the way to south to Manchester, and then west to Southport and Liverpool.

Like so many operators Ribble grew in the years following World War I; the company was formed in 1919 and expanded naturally and by acquisition. The fleet had topped the 1,000 mark by the mid-1930s, and in 1970 totalled 1,026 vehicles (517 double-deck, 304 single-deck, 282 coaches – including 20 double-deck coaches). Its operations were widely varied and the bus fleet reflected this. There were deep rural operations in

Westmorland, trunk services throughout the network, and intensive urban services in places like Carlisle, Fleetwood and Preston, and even Liverpool, with services north to Crosby and Southport. Many of Ribble's services were operated jointly with municipal and independent operators.

Overlaid on this was Ribble's massive commitment to coaching, with its own and joint express services and programmes of day and extended tours.

Express services took Ribble coaches throughout the north-west, into Scotland, and into other parts of England, often joint with local operators. And there was the Standerwick operation; W C Standerwick Ltd was taken over in 1932 and the name was retained for certain limited stop and express services, notably those to London. Ribble was also a member of the Yorkshire-Blackpool Services pool, along with Yorkshire-based fellow NBC companies. As the name suggests, these provided links between Yorkshire towns and Blackpool.

Based in Preston, it is hardly surprising that Ribble traditionally turned to the products of nearby Leyland Motors for the great majority of its bus fleet. In 1970 the only non-Leylands in the fleet were 17 Albion Lowlanders – Leylands in all but name – and 61 Bristols. The Bristols were RELL buses – some at least had Leyland engines. Previously, the Leopard had been the company's standard single-deck purchase in the 1960s, in short and long bus and coach forms. Double-deckers were

Leyland Titan PD2 and PD3 types, and Atlanteans.

Just as Leylands dominated the Ribble fleet, Leylands outnumbered other types by a ratio of four to one in the municipal bus fleets of north Lancashire. And although locally-built East Lancs bodies could be found in many fleets, builders like Crossley, Leyland, Metro-Cammell and Northern Counties also featured.

The other NBC fleet in the north-west was Cumberland Motor Services, a former Tilling Group company that was set up in 1921 when the British Automobile Traction company acquired a half share in the Whitehaven Motor Service, adopting the Cumberland name. It expanded in the 1920s, and, following the acquisition of an interest in the company by the LMS railway company in 1930, proceeded to acquire local operators. Tilling & BAT held another third, with the balance in the hands of the Meageen family. In the 1942 restructuring of the Tilling and BET groups, Cumberland became a Tilling Group company, though it was some time before Tilling standard vehicle types joined the Leyland-dominated fleet.

The Cumberland company's territory in 1970 covered the area west of a line drawn from Carlisle to Millom, and included the main towns of Whitehaven, Workington and Cockermouth. Trunk services linked these towns to Carlisle and Keswick, the fringes of Ribble territory.

The Cumberland fleet in 1970 still included some Leylands but was inevitably dominated by Bristol/ECW products. There were 193 vehicles – 95 double-deckers, 84 single-deckers and 14 coaches. Unusual for a Tilling fleet were Bedford/Duple coaches. The fleet included Bristol/ECW MWs, REs, LHs, and Lodekkas of the LD, FS and FLF varieties. The newest

deliveries in 1970 were RELL6L and LH6P buses, delivered that year. In 1972 Cumberland would receive the first Leyland National to enter service, symbolic because of the Leyland National plant outside Workington.

Looking at the municipal fleets in the north-west in 1970, we start with the slightly isolated Barrow Corporation system, serving the important industrial and shipbuilding town. The corporation came later into public transport, although the progression had been a typical one in the north – horse bus, steam tram, electric tram. The steam tram system had been bought by British Electric Traction (BET) in 1899 and the electric tramway network was sold to the corporation in 1920. Barrow had run motorbuses and these had replaced the trams by 1932. The fleet was largely dominated by Leylands, and the 1970 fleet (59 buses: 31 double-deck, 28 single-deck) included Titans, Tiger Cubs and Leopards. The newest deliveries were two-door East Lancs-bodied Leopards, new in 1969, and Barrow would go on to buy single-deck Daimler Fleetlines and Leyland Nationals in the early 1970s.

Heading south, the next municipal fleet in 1970 was Morecambe & Heysham Corporation. With two towns and two separate horse tramway operations, the early history is more complex than is usually the case, but horse trams survived as late as 1926, to be replaced by motorbuses, and there were also petrol-driven trams on one section of the network. The Morecambe and Heysham undertakings came together in 1929.

Unlike most local municipalities, Morecambe & Heysham was not a big Leyland fan, preferring AECs – Regents and Swifts. Its 1970 fleet comprised 50 buses (40 double-deck, 10 single-deck), and the newest deliveries were Northern Counties-bodied two-

Opposite left: At Ribble's northern frontier, at Carlisle, one of the 50 Saunders-Roe-bodied Leyland Tiger Cub PSUC1/1 44-seaters supplied in 1953/54.
Edward Shirras

Right: Representing a change of direction for Ribble, a 1969 Bristol RELL6G with two-door ECW 41-seat standee body, on a Kendal local service.
Edward Shirras

Above: Looking slightly uneasy in Ribble livery at Carlisle, a former United Auto 1958 Bristol MW5G with 45-seat ECW body, one of 24 vehicles transferred to Ribble in January 1969 with United's Carlisle operations.
Iain MacGregor

Left: Ribble was, perhaps unsurprisingly, a long-standing fan of locally-built Leyland chassis, and this bus is an all-Lancashire product, a 1967 Atlantean PDR1/2 with 72-seat Wigan-built Northern Counties body, seen at Blackpool after working in on the X8 Great Harwood-Blackpool service.
Geoff Lumb

door Swifts, although it would go on to Seddon Pennine RUs in 1972/73.

Nearby was Lancaster Corporation, which had started with electric trams in 1903; motorbuses had been used since 1917 and the last trams ran in 1930. The 1970 fleet (36 buses: 11 double-deck, 25 single-deck) was dominated by Leylands – Titans, Tiger Cubs and Leopards – with the newest deliveries being East Lancs-bodied Leopards delivered in 1969/70. Lancaster went on to buy more Leopards and then Nationals, and in 1974 the newly-defined City of Lancaster included Morecambe & Heysham, so the transport undertakings were merged into the new Lancaster City Transport.

Continuing south down the coast, the next undertaking is the sizeable Blackpool Corporation, with in 1970 115 trams and 150 buses (135 double-deck, 15 single-deck). Blackpool was the scene of the first electric street tramway in Britain, in 1885, adding its first buses in 1921. Although much of the tramway system has been abandoned, the famous Fleetwood-Starr Gate

Left: Cumberland came later to Bristol/ECW products than most other Tilling Group companies, but by the mid-1960s the Tilling influence was obvious. This 1965 Bristol FLF6G with 70-seat ECW forward entrance body is seen in Carlisle in the summer of 1970.
Mark Page

Centre: Barrow Corporation was another Leyland fan, and this smart 1958 Titan PD240 has 61-seat Park Royal bodywork.
Mark Page

Below: Morecambe & Heysham favoured AEC chassis, and this is a 1970 delivery, a Swift 2MP2R with two-door Northern Counties 50-seat body.
Geoff Lumb

tramway survives. The 1970 bus fleet was dominated by Metro-Cammell-bodied Leyland Titan PD2s and PD3s, though the most recent purchases were two-door Marshall-bodied AEC Swifts, in 1969/70. Many more Swifts would be bought in 1971/74.

Adjacent to Blackpool is Lytham St Annes, where the local corporation transport undertaking had been formed in 1922 when the separate Lytham and St Annes councils were merged. St Annes had run electric trams to the boundary with Blackpool, with running powers into the centre of the town. Lytham St Annes abandoned its trams in 1937. The 37-strong 1970 bus fleet (30 double-deck, seven single-deck) was 100 per cent Leyland, Titans and Tiger Cubs, and its newest buses were two-door Northern Counties-bodied Panthers, delivered in 1969, and Northern Counties-bodied Atlanteans, bought in 1970.

Inland from Lytham St Annes is the important town of Preston, where the corporation had a fleet of 94 buses in 1970 (79 double-deck, 15 single-deck). Preston's early urban transport history was typical of so many towns – company horse trams running on track leased from the corporation, municipal acquisition in 1900, electrification from 1904, motorbuses from 1922, last trams in 1935.

With Leyland Motors a few miles down the road, Leylands dominated the Preston fleet; in 1970 Preston was an all-Leyland fleet, with Titans, Tiger Cubs and Leopards. Like so many other municipalities, Preston went for significant batches of two-door single-deckers in the late 1960s – in this case Panthers with Metro-Cammell and Marshall bodies in 1968-70. It would go on to buy more Panthers in 1971/72 and bought five ex-Stratford Blue examples from Midland Red in 1971.

East from Preston you reach Blackburn, where company-owned steam tramways from 1881 passed to the corporation in

1889, who electrified the system. Tramway abandonment was completed in 1949, and motorbuses – Leylands, of course – were used from 1929. The 1970 fleet of 105 (85 double-deck, 20 single-deck) comprised 56 Leylands and 49 Guys. Bodies on 84 of the buses was by East Lancs, based in the town. The buses were mainly Leyland Titans and Guy Arabs, but in 1968 Blackburn bought its first Atlanteans and in 1969 a batch of Tiger Cubs. More Atlanteans would be bought from 1971, along with some Seddon Pennine RUs.

Just south of Blackburn is Darwen, and the two transport undertakings were closely linked. The company steam trams that served Blackburn also served Darwen and that system was jointly acquired by the two corporations. Darwen abandoned electric trams in 1946, and had operated motorbuses since 1926. The 1970 fleet of 32 buses (27 double-deck, five single-deck) was mainly of Leyland manufacture, Titans and Tiger Cubs; the newest Titans were delivered in 1969, with forward entrance East Lancs bodies.

East of Blackburn is Accrington, again with company-operated steam trams (from 1886), passing to the corporation (1907), who proceeded to electrify the system; trams last ran in 1932. Motorbuses appeared in 1928, and by 1970 there were 52 of them (39 double-deck, 13 single-deck) fairly evenly divided between Guys and Leylands, with five Bristol RESL6L thrown

in for good measure. Bodywork was all by East Lancs. Although Accrington had bought the Bristol single-deckers in 1968/69, it also bought Leyland Atlanteans and would go on to buy more in the early 1970s.

North-west of Accrington is Burnley, and beyond that town are Nelson and Colne. In 1933 the transport undertakings of the three towns were brought together as the Burnley, Colne & Nelson Joint Transport Committee. The three towns ran buses and trams, although by 1935 the tramway system had been abandoned.

The Burnley Colne & Nelson fleet in 1970 consisted of 138 buses (74 double-deck, 64 single-deck), mostly Leyland with some Bristols and Guys. The Leylands were Titans, Tiger Cubs, Leopards and Panthers, with a handful of long-lived Tiger PS2s. The newest buses in 1970 were Northern Counties-bodied Bristol RESL6L bought in 1969, and there would be further batches of RESLs as well as Seddon RUs and Leyland Nationals over the next few years. Bodywork tended to be built in Lancashire – mainly by East Lancs, but also by Leyland and Northern Counties.

At Lower Mosley Street bus station, Manchester, two Ribble express services meet. On the left is a 1963 Leyland Leopard PSU3/3RT with Harrington Cavalier 49-seat body on the X53 to Burnley, alongside a 1962 Leyland Atlantean PDR1/1 with Metro-Cammell 78-seat body, on the X3 to Great Harwood.
M Fowler

The remaining municipal operator in the area in 1970, south of Accrington and Burnley, was the Rossendale Joint Transport Committee, itself a fairly recent entity. In 1968 it had assumed control for the bus services provided by the corporation fleets at Haslingden and Rawtenstall. Haslingden and Rawtenstall had been served by the same steam tramway that served Accrington and Darwen, and bought their shares in 1907. Electric trams then served Haslingden and Rawtenstall, but these were provided by Accrington and Rawtenstall; Haslingden continued to own its track. The Haslingden route closed in 1930, and the Rawtenstall route in 1932.

Haslingden and Rawtenstall were both early motorbus operators, in 1907, and in the postwar years there were close links between the two undertakings, and with Ramsbottom UDC. Rossendale JTC was set up in April 1968 and in 1970 had a fleet of 55 buses (43 double-deck, 12 single-deck). All the chassis were Leylands, with bodies by Leyland and East Lancs. The newest buses in 1970 were East Lancs-bodied Leopards, bought in 1968, and this combination continued to be delivered in the early 1970s.

The principal independent bus operator in the north-west was J Fishwick & Sons of Leyland. This famous, long-established company dates back to 1907, and built up a network of services in Leyland and Preston, perhaps inevitably using locally-built Leyland products. The proximity of Fishwick to the Leyland plants meant that over the years the fleet has included some unusual types, as well as former demonstrators.

The 1970 Fishwick fleet (44 vehicles: 17 double-deck,

16 single-deck, 11 coaches) was 40 Leylands, plus two Albion, one Bedford and one Austin coach. The Leylands included Tiger Cubs, Leopards, a Panther, Titans and Atlanteans, and the newest bus deliveries, in 1970, were three Leopards bodied locally by Fowler. More Atlanteans would follow in the early 1970s, along with single-deck Leyland Fleetlines (with Leyland engines) and Leopard coaches.

The structure of the bus industry in the north-west of England in 1970 has barely survived into the 21st century. The once-strong group of municipal operations has all but disappeared. Only Blackpool and Rossendale remained in local authority control early in 2007. Blackburn, and Burnley Colne & Nelson, were in the Transdev Blazefield grouping. Lytham St Annes (later Fylde) was acquired by Blackpool Transport in 1994; Darwen was merged into Blackburn Borough Transport in 1974; Accrington (later Hyndburn) and Barrow went to Stagecoach; and Preston, uniquely, went to its management and employees.

In the National Bus Company sell-off Cumberland went to Stagecoach in 1987 and Ribble to its management team in 1988, though it too passed to Stagecoach. ∎

Lancaster bought two small batches of Leyland Titan PD2/37 with East Lancs 65-seat forward entrance bodies in the 1960s. This bus, new in 1963, is surrounded by other buses from the Lancaster fleet, including a Crossley-rebodied utility Daimler, on the right, and an ex-Rochdale Corporation AEC Regal IV/Burlingham, on the left.
Geoff Lumb

Blackpool bought a substantial fleet of Metro-Cammell Orion-bodied Leyland Titans between 1957 and 1968. This is a 1962 PD3/1 with full-fronted 73-seat body; from 1965 deliveries had a more conventional front end, like the bus behind.
Geoff Lumb

Lytham St Annes bought this full-fronted Leyland Titan PD2/21 with Metro-Cammell 59-seat body from nearby Blackpool in 1970.
Geoff Lumb

Above: Preston Corporation rebuilt some of its Leyland-bodied Titan PD2/10 fleet between 1959 and 1965 to produce 30ft-long PD3/6 types with 70-seat forward entrance bodies. No.51, seen in Preston bus station, started life in 1954 and was rebuilt in 1963. Some of the rebuilding included converting lowbridge buses to full-height.
Iain MacGregor

Below: Blackburn was unusual among Lancashire municipalities in favouring Guys as well as Leylands. This is a 1961 Johannesburg-fronted Guy Arab IV with locally-built East Lancs 63-seat body, one of a batch of 12.
Iain MacGregor

Above: Ribble built up a substantial fleet of Marshall-bodied Leyland Leopards in the 1960s, later deliveries being of the shorter PSU4/4R variety, like no.670, seen here.
Edward Shirras

Left: Unusual-looking buses in the Ribble fleet were the 16 Leyland-Albion Lowlander LR1 with full-fronted Alexander 72-seat bodies, bought in 1965/66.
Edward Shirras

Ribble coaches were familiar throughout Britain. Here a Leyland Leopard L2 with Plaxton Panorama body, one of two bought from Michelin, is parked alongside a 1959 Leyland Atlantean PDR1/1 with 50-seat Weymann coach body from the associated Standerwick fleet.
Edward Shirras

A reminder of Cumberland's former fondness for Leyland chassis is provided by this 1953 Royal Tiger PSU1/13 with ECW body, transferred from its fellow Tilling Group fleet, United Auto.
Edward Shirras

Cumberland bought over 50 Bristol RELL6L between 1967 and 1972, the majority with 53-seat ECW bodies, like this 1968 example.
Edward Shirras

Above: The Darwen fleet was dominated by Leylands, the newest being East Lancs-bodied PD2s and PD3s. This is a 1964 PD3A/1 with forward entrance 72-seat body.
Iain MacGregor

Below: Accrington's newest single-deckers in 1970 were Bristol RESL6L with 43-seat East Lancs bodywork like this 1968 example wearing the corporation's distinctive livery.
Iain MacGregor

Like so many municipal operators in the north-west, Burnley Colne & Nelson favoured East Lancs-bodied Leylands, like this 1953 Titan PD2/12 57-seater.
Ted Jones

Right: In 1970 Rossendale had a 100 per cent Leyland fleet, including this 1968 Leopard PSU4/2R with 46-seat East Lancs body.
Geoff Lumb

Below: The famous Leyland-based independent, Fishwick, mainly operated locally-bought Leylands, including some more unusual variants like this rare 1957 Leyland-MCW Olympian 44-seater.
Iain MacGregor

The Lancaster fleet included single-deckers like this 1958 Leyland Tiger Cub PSUC1/3 with 43-seat East Lancs body.
Edward Shirras

Right: In 1969 Lytham St Annes bought three of these Leyland Panther PSUR1A/1R with two-door Northern Counties 49-seat bodies.

Below: Blackburn contrast – a newly-delivered 1968 Leyland Atlantean PDR1/1 with 76-seat East Lancs body is passed by a 1949 Guy Arab III with 56-seat Crossley body.
T W Moore

Above: Accrington's first Leyland Atlanteans were three PDR1A/1 examples delivered in 1969 with 78-seat East Lancs bodies.
David R Harman

Below: Fishwick had this Leyland Tiger Cub PSUC1/12 bodied by the local firm, Fowler, in 1969. The company went on to take five Daimler Fleetline single-deckers and a Leyland Atlantean double-decker with bodies by the same manufacturer.
M A Penn

# Greater Manchester and Cheshire

Selnec PTE inherited a very mixed selection of buses when it was set up in 1969. In Lancashire, Leylands inevitably dominated, but some constituent fleets favoured AECs. This is a former Leigh Corporation 1967 AEC Renown with 72-seat forward entrance East Lancs body, newly painted in the PTE's distinctive livery.
Iain MacGregor

Although Greater Manchester was only formally set up as a metropolitan county in 1974, the idea of a Manchester conurbation authority had been around for some time. There were plans in the 1960s to create a new county, including a 1969 report proposing a new Selnec (South-east Lancashire, north-east Cheshire) county. This would have covered much the same area as the later Greater Manchester, as well as places like Macclesfield and Warrington. Although this didn't happen, the Selnec Passenger Transport Authority (PTA) was set up in 1969, working through the Selnec Passenger Transport Executive (PTE).

The creation of Selnec PTE had seen substantial changes to the structure of public transport in the area around Manchester. No fewer than 11 municipal transport undertakings disappeared into the Selnec pot, ranging from mighty Manchester, with 1,258 buses, to tiny Ramsbottom UDC (12 buses). The others, in order of 1969 fleet size, were Salford (276), Bolton (252), Oldham (200), Stockport (162), Rochdale (131), Bury (96), SHMD Board (91), Ashton-under-Lyne (60), and Leigh (58). With 2,700 buses in 1970, this was a giant undertaking, by far the largest of the four PTEs set up in 1969/70.

The 1970 'Little Red Book' entry for Selnec lists six types of bus chassis – AEC, Bedford, Bristol, Daimler, Dennis and Leyland – and 13 bodybuilders – Alexander, Burlingham, Crossley, East Lancs, Leyland, Marshall, MCW, Northern Counties, Park Royal, Plaxton, Roe, Seddon and Willowbrook. And as every municipality had its own views on the ideal vehicle, Selnec would have to embark quickly on a standardisation policy.

This of course it would do, but in 1970 it was still trying to fuse 11 very different undertakings together and impose a new company culture. It also found itself committed to receiving deliveries of buses that had been ordered in municipal days, which only compounded the problem, although some orders were adapted to produce the prototypes of the new standard types.

Above: A former Bury Corporation Leyland Atlantean PDR1/1 with Liverpool-style Metro-Cammell 74-seat body, dating from 1963, is pursued by a fine Albion truck.

Iain MacGregor

Below: Manchester Corporation was the largest component of the initial Selnec PTE fleet, mainly contributing Daimlers and Leylands. This is a 1963 Daimler CCG6K with Metro-Cammell 65-seat body, newly painted in Selnec livery. It carried the blue Central fleetname style, while the former Bury and Leigh buses on these pages carry magenta Northern logos.

Iain MacGregor

Selnec was made up of 11 different municipal operators, each with its own distinct vehicle-buying policy. Although Leylands dominated, there was a range of different types, and bodywork often reflected local preferences. This is a 1969 Atlantean PDR1A/1 with Northern Counties 71-seat body as delivered to Ashton in 1969, before the PTE was formally established. M J Fenton

Delivered to Selnec in 1970 were Metro-Cammell-bodied Leyland Atlanteans ordered by Manchester and Salford; Metro-Cammell- and Park Royal-bodied Daimler Fleetlines ordered by Manchester; Roe-bodied Atlanteans ordered by Oldham; Northern Counties-bodied Atlanteans ordered by Ashton; Seddon-bodied AEC Swifts ordered by Rochdale; East Lancs-bodied Fleetlines ordered by Bury; and East Lancs-bodied Atlanteans ordered by Bolton.

Selnec's massive operating area covered hundreds of square miles of Lancashire and Cheshire, stretching from Ramsbottom in the north to Wilmslow in the south, and from Leigh in the west to Glossop in the east.

Selnec quickly adopted an orange/white livery – the liveries of the previous fleets covered reds, greens and blues – and started to apply this to its massive fleet. Other buses received vinyls on their existing liveries. Selnec was probably the most image-conscious of the early PTEs, applying its corporate style imaginatively on vehicles and publicity. It had also inherited some of the most striking double-deckers on the road, the ex-Manchester Mancunian-style Atlanteans and Fleetlines, and would go on to develop a standard double-deck design that would be refined over the next 14 years.

But Selnec was not the only bus operator in the area. NBC's North Western and Ribble companies had a significant involvement, running services within and into the PTE area. There were also services from Yorkshire.

There was one significant independent presence within the Selnec area – Lancashire United Transport. LUT's origins are in tramways, which were replaced by trolleybuses from 1930; the last South Lancs trolleybuses ran in 1958. But LUT had also experimented with motorbuses, first in 1906 and then again in 1914, but from 1919 the company's use of buses expanded. LUT's operating area was immediately west of Manchester, centred on Atherton.

In 1970 the LUT fleet totalled 396 buses and coaches (249

double-deck, 107 single-deck, 40 coaches), making it the largest independent operator in the UK. The LUT fleet included a range of different chassis types, dominated by Guy with 189 examples; Northern Counties bodies were particularly popular. The newest LUT buses in 1970 were two-door Northern Counties-bodied Bristol LH6Ls and Daimler Fleetlines, and Plaxton-bodied Seddon RUs.

LUT had joint services with Bolton, Salford and Leigh corporations, and these continued under Selnec. Agreement was soon reached with Selnec on service and fare co-ordination, and over the next few years the two organisations became closer, leading to the acquisition of LUT by Greater Manchester PTE in 1976.

The other notable independent in the Manchester area was considerably smaller, but it had a high profile, with services into the centre of Manchester. A Mayne & Son Ltd was established in 1920, soon starting services on the Ashton New Road. Under the PTE, Mayne continued to expand, and survives in 2007. In 1970 it had a fleet of 29 (14 double-deckers, 15 coaches), and for its bus fleet favoured AECs with Park Royal bodies, the newest bought in 1965.

Selnec PTE only lasted in its original form until 1974 when Greater Manchester Metropolitan County was set up, and Greater Manchester PTE was created. The new county had different boundaries, which took in Wigan, so the municipal fleet became part of the new Greater Manchester Buses operation. Wigan Corporation acquired the local steam tramway

Ordered by Bury Corporation but delivered new to Selnec, a 1970 Daimler Fleetline CRG6LX with East Lancs 73-seat body. It was delivered in Selnec livery.
David Barrow

company in 1902 and electrified the system. It also ran trolleybuses between 1925 and 1931. It bought its first buses in 1919 and in 1970 its fleet consisted of 151 buses (137 double-deck, 14 single-deck), all Leyland chassis with bodies by Leyland itself, or by the two Wigan coachbuilders, Massey and Northern Counties. Wigan's newest deliveries in 1970 were two-door Northern Counties-bodied Leyland Atlanteans and Panthers.

At the time when the PTAs were selling off their bus companies, Greater Manchester Transport was split into two parts, GM Buses North and GM Buses South, and these were sold to their employees in 1994. Two years later they were bought out by the big groups – North to First and South to Stagecoach.

In 1970 bus operations in Cheshire were provided by the NBC's North Western Road Car, but another major NBC company had a significant presence, and indeed had its headquarters in the county town, Chester. Crosville of course had a major presence in North Wales, and so has been covered in the Midlands and Wales book in this series. Its English bus operations took it south to Crewe and to the fringes of Staffordshire, and it had urban operations to the north, on Merseyside.

North Western's origins date back to 1913 when the British Automobile Traction company started operation in Macclesfield, but in 1923 the North Western company was formed, and its head office soon relocated to Stockport. As with most of the territorial operators, the railway companies bought into North Western in 1930, and when the Tilling and BET group companies were reorganised in 1942, it became a BET Group company. Much of North Western's business came from the Manchester area, and it had garages in the new Selnec area at places like Altrincham, Glossop, Manchester, Oldham and Stockport.

North Western's 1970 fleet comprised 552 buses and coaches (188 double-deck, 279 single-deck, 85 coaches). These were almost even numbers of AECs and Leylands, plus significant batches of Bristols, Daimlers and Dennises. Bodywork was a typical BET mix, with significant numbers of Alexander and Willowbrook products. Its newest buses in 1970 were Alexander-bodied Bristol RELL6Gs.

North Western's presence in Selnec territory would lead to the company's dismemberment in 1972. Parts were transferred to other NBC fleets – Crosville, Trent and National Travel (North-West) – but 250 of its buses and five garages passed to Selnec, and a new Selnec fleetname – Cheshire – appeared.

One other municipal operator that was beyond the reach of the new Selnec PTE was Chester Corporation. Chester had a small horse tram system from 1879, which passed into municipal control in 1902, leading to electrification the following year. Motorbuses were first bought in 1930, replacing the trams in that year.

The 1970 Chester fleet consisted of 51 buses (47 double-deck, four single-deck), mostly Guys with Massey bodies. The newest deliveries in 1970 had been Northern Counties-bodied Daimler Fleetlines, but as late as 1969 Chester had been buying Northern Counties-bodied Guy Arab Vs. The Chester City Transport fleet was one of the reducing number of fleets still in local authority control in the 21st century, but in 2006 the undertaking was offered for sale. ∎

Above: With such a large fleet, it took some time to repaint everything into Selnec colours, and for some time the only external evidence of the new ownership was the new fleet number and legal lettering. Later, fleetnames and logos were removed and replaced by Selnec vinyls on buses still carrying the colours of their original owners. This Salford Leyland Atlantean PDR1A/1 with two-door Park Royal 72-seat body, carries its new Selnec fleetnumber; it was previously Salford no.321.
Iain MacGregor

Left: Bolton Corporation had operated a varied fleet, and its last new buses before the creation of Selnec were 15 Leyland Atlantean PDR1A/1 with this unique style of East Lancs 72-seat two-door bodywork.
Iain MacGregor

Heading a queue of similar buses at the Stockport stand at Manchester's Piccadilly bus station, an ex-Stockport 1967 Leyland Titan PD2/40 with 64-seat East Lancs body. The bus behind, in Selnec colours, has the green Southern fleetname.
Kevin Lane

Formerly no.1 in the tiny Ramsbottom UDC fleet, this 1961 Leyland Titan PD2/24 with 63-seat East Lancs body carries its new Selnec fleetnumber, and Selnec advertising, as it sits in front of a former Bury Leyland PD3/6 with Weymann 73-seat body.
Kevin Lane

Rochdale Corporation had favoured AECs and latterly Daimlers, and this 1965 Fleetline CRG6LX with 77-seat Weymann body is at Ashton bus station in Selnec colours.
Geoff Lumb

Although the initial Selnec fleet was dominated by double-deckers, several constituent fleets had growing fleets of single-deckers. This is a 1968 Leigh Corporation Leyland Leopard PSU4/2R with East Lancs body.
C B Golding

With 11 once-separate undertakings involved, there were inevitably new buses on order that were not ready for delivery until the formation of Selnec. This Oldham-ordered Leyland Atlantean PDR1A/1 with Roe 74-seat body was one of six delivered in 1970 in Oldham colours but with Selnec fleetnumber and legal lettering; these were the first new buses for Selnec Southern.
R L Wilson

Selnec inherited over 100 Leyland Atlanteans from Bolton Corporation, including this 1968 PDR1/1 with 78-seat East Lancs body, seen just at the time the PTE was set up.
Like Manchester, Bolton was concerned about the appearance of its buses and had adopted this brighter livery application for its newer fleet.
R L Wilson

Above: The newest deliveries to SHMD Board before Selnec, were 10 of these Walsall-style short Daimler Fleetline CRG6LW with Northern Counties 68-seat two-door bodies.
E N Pounder

Below: Although Salford also bought Atlanteans, it simultaneously built up a fleet of around 100 of these Metro-Cammell-bodied forward entrance Leyland Titan PD2/40 between 1963 and 1967.
M C Beamish

A former Leigh Corporation 1953 AEC Regent III with East Lancs 53-seat lowbridge body, still in full Leigh livery but with Selnec fleetnumber, sits alongside an ex-Leigh Leyland PD2/East Lancs in full Selnec regalia.
Kevin Lane

The Mayne's livery brought a touch of variety to the Manchester scene. This is a 1962 AEC Regent V 2D3RA with East Lancs 73-seat body.
Mark Page

Still wearing Oldham Corporation's later pommard/cream livery, a 1959 Leyland Titan PD2/30 with 65-seat body sits at Rochdale, with the headquarters of Yelloway, the well-known express coach operator, in-the background.
Iain MacGregor

Freshly repainted, a 1962 Lancashire United Guy Arab IV/ Northern Counties sits outside the company's central works at Howe Bridge, Atherton.
Mark Page

Lancashire United continued to buy Guy Arabs until 1967. This is a 1966 Arab V/ Northern Counties 73-seater, in Warrington.
Iain MacGregor

The conductor rests against the front nearside wing of a Wigan Corporation 1966 Leyland Titan PD2/37 with Northern Counties 64-seat forward entrance bodywork, built in the town.
Royston Morgan

Above: Manchester City Transport's Mancunian double-deck design was the first specifically designed for driver-only operation, and set a trend with its squarer lines and brighter livery. Photographed just a few months before Selnec was set up, a 1968 Leyland Atlantean PDR1/1 with Park Royal 73-seat body in Chorlton, is not really making best use of the Manchester three-box destination display.
Edward Shirras

Below: The orange Selnec livery appeared on an amazing range of buses from the constituent fleets. This is a former Leigh Corporation Leyland Titan PD3A/3 with East Lancs lowbridge 66-seat body, seen in its former hometown.
C B Golding

Selnec opened its new Stockport garage in 1970, and a Selnec-liveried former Stockport 1958 Leyland Titan PD2/30 with locally-built Crossley 61-seat body, sits centre stage against a backdrop of ex-Stockport Titans, still in Stockport colours.
Eric B Simpson

Buses ordered by the former municipals continued to be delivered in 1971, though by this time they appeared in Selnec livery, like this Oldham-ordered Roe-bodied Leyland Atlantean PDR1A/1, seen in Ashton.
C B Golding

A taste of what was to come was provided with the construction in 1970/71 of six experimental double-deckers, EX1-6, built on Leyland Atlantean PDR1A/1 chassis that had been ordered by Ashton. The Northern Counties 75-seat one-door bodies were the first of a basic design that would appear on over 1,700 Atlanteans and Daimler Fleetlines over the next decade. Although the body design is less dramatic than the Mancunian in the background, it has a timeless appeal, and the adoption of a Manchester-style destination display will be noted.
K Walker

Massey and Northern Counties were both based in Wigan and the local corporation bought from both bodybuilders. This is a 1959 Leyland Titan PD3/2 with 72-seat forward entrance Massey body.
Mark Page

In 1970 the writing was on the wall for North Western as an important territorial NBC company; in 1972 its services within Greater Manchester would pass to Selnec, along with some 250 vehicles, and the rest would be divided between Crosville, Trent and National Travel (North-West). This 1970 Buxton view shows a 1963 AEC Reliance 2U3RA with Willowbrook 53-seat body.
Mark Page

In its last years, North Western bought a number of Bristol RELL6G with Alexander 49-seat Y type bodies. This one is at Whaley Bridge in 1969.
Omnicolour/Martin Llewellyn

Above: North Western required lowheight double-deckers and in the 1960s bought Dennis Lolines, AEC Renowns and Daimler Fleetlines. This Renown 3B3RA with 72-seat Park Royal body was new in 1964 and would pass to Selnec in 1972.

Iain MacGregor

Below: Guy Arabs were a popular choice in several fleets in the north-west, including Chester Corporation, which continued to buy Arabs until 1969. This is a 1961 Arab IV with Johannesburg-style front and Massey 73-seat forward entrance body, in Eastgate in 1970.

Mark Page

Above: A 42-seat Plaxton-bodied Bristol RESL6G with Plaxton 42-seat two-door body delivered to Lancashire United in 1967.
Gavin Booth

Left: Sitting at the terminus of Mayne's 213 route, at Droylsden in 1970, a 1961 AEC Regent V 2D3RA with rather ungainly Park Royal 73-seat body.
R C Chapman

North Western's last new double-deckers were Alexander-bodied Daimler Fleetline CRG6LX 75-seaters like this 1964 example, which would pass to Selnec in 1972.
Edward Shirras

In 1964 North Western bought 10 unusual Bedford VAL14 with Strachans 52-seat bodies with special roof profiles to allow them to pass under Dunham Woodhouses Bridge on the Bridgewater Canal. One is seen in Altrincham.
Edward Shirras

The last Guy Arabs delivered to a UK operator were three Arab V with Northern Counties 73-seat forward entrance bodies, new in 1969 to Chester Corporation. Numerically the last, no.47 is seen in 1970.
Edward Shirras

# Merseyside

In 1969 Merseyside Passenger Transport Authority acquired the assets of the municipal transport departments of Birkenhead, Liverpool and Wallasey. The new Merseyside Passenger Transport Executive operated some 1,000 buses over an area stretching from Formby and Ormskirk in the north to the Mersey in the south and also taking in the Wirral peninsula.

The three constituents of the new PTE had long connections with street transport. Birkenhead was the site of Britain's first horse tramway, in 1860, and the corporation assumed full control of the system, which was electrified in 1901. The corporation's first motorbuses ran in 1919 and the trams were withdrawn by 1937. The first tramway in Wallasey opened in 1879 and the Urban District Council took it over in 1901, electrifying it the following year. The last tram ran in 1933, and buses had been operated since 1920. As Wallasey grew, the UDC became a borough in 1910 and a county borough in 1913.

As with Selnec, one undertaking dominated the new PTE, and this was Liverpool. There had been horse trams in Liverpool since 1869, full control passing to the corporation in 1897, with electric cars following the next year. A substantial electric tramway network was developed, but this had been abandoned by 1957. Motorbuses started in 1911, but only really came into their own after the start of the tramway abandonment.

The fleets of the PTE's constituent operators in 1969 had been 1,132 at Liverpool, 227 at Birkenhead and 75 at Wallasey.

The PTE bus operations were split into three divisions; North and South covered Liverpool and Wirral covered the former Birkenhead and Wallasey fleets. At first there were separate liveries: Liverpool buses retained their traditional green, while the Wirral livery took elements of the previous liveries, using blue and primrose. Later a standard livery of Verona Green and Buttermilk would be used for all buses.

Left: With the creation of Merseyside PTE, Liverpool's buses initially retained their normal livery, with the new PTE logo and legal lettering. Delivered new to the PTE in 1970 was this Bristol VRT/LH6G with 80-seat two-door East Lancs bodywork, the first of a batch of 60 buses.
Omnicolour/Chris Aston

Right: Buses in Merseyside's Wirral division wore a blue/cream livery that reflected the colours of the Birkenhead and Wallasey Corporation fleets. A newly-repainted ex-Wallasey Leyland Atlantean PDR1/1 with Metro-Cammell 77-seat body, from that undertaking's pioneering batch delivered in 1958/59, sits in front of a 1951 Leyland Titan PD2/1 with Metro-Cammell 56-seat body, still in Wallasey colours.
Geoff Lumb

The initial fleet was inevitably dominated by Liverpool buses from the substantial fleet of Metro-Cammell-bodied Leyland Atlanteans bought in the 1960s, as well as older AECs and Leylands. Liverpool had also embraced single-deck buses in a big way in the late 1960s, so there were two-door Metro-Cammell-bodied Leyland Panthers and Park Royal-bodied Bristol RELL6Gs, some delivered new to the PTE.

The Birkenhead and Wallasey fleets both donated Leyland Titans and Atlanteans, and Birkenhead also had Daimler Fleetlines. An interesting Atlantean from the Wallasey fleet was FHF 451, one of the first four production Atlanteans dating from 1958.

The newest deliveries to Birkenhead before the formation of the PTE were two-door Northern Counties-bodied Atlanteans, and more, ordered by the corporation, would be delivered in 1970/71. Also on order and delivered to the PTE were unusual Northern Counties two-door-bodied Leyland Atlantean single-deckers.

Although it inherited a less mixed fleet than Selnec had, Merseyside also set about ordering substantial batches of new standard buses, partly to take advantage of the new Bus Grants scheme. Alexander-bodied Atlanteans were in course of delivery in 1970 and this combination would continue to be favoured until 1984. Also delivered in 1970/71 were East Lancs-bodied Bristol VRTs, and others would follow in 1974/75. The Wirral division would receive Daimler Fleetlines in 1973.

Further boundary changes in 1974 would enlarge the PTE's area and bring two further municipalities into the fold, St Helens and Southport.

In 1970, though, these were still trading as normal. St Helens had horse then steam trams and the corporation bought the system in 1897, which was leased to another company until 1911. From 1899 electric trams were introduced and trolleybuses replaced them between 1927 and 1936. Motorbuses were first introduced in 1923 and the last trolleybus ran in 1958.

The 1970 St Helens fleet of 127 buses was made up of 94 double-deck, 32 single-deck and one coach. AEC and Leyland chassis were favoured, with bodywork mainly by East Lancs,

Metro-Cammell and Marshall. What had been a largely double-deck fleet changed direction in 1968 when the first batch of two-door Marshall-bodied AEC Swifts was bought, followed by others in 1969/71, and then in 1972-75. Some were delivered new to the PTE.

Southport had horse trams from 1873 and electric trams from 1900, and these lasted until 1934. Motorbuses were bought from 1924 and the 1970 fleet comprised 59 (44 double-deck, 15 single-deck). Although the fleet included some elderly open-top Leyland Tigers and Titans for seafront services – and these would pass to Merseyside PTE – the newest buses in 1970 were two-door Metro-Cammell-bodied Leyland Panthers, and more Panthers would be bought in 1971.

Merseyside PTE adopted the Merseybus name at the time of deregulation, in 1986, and Merseyside Transport Ltd was sold to its employees in 1992. This in turn was sold to Arriva in the year 2000.

Beyond the scope of Merseyside PTE were the municipal operations at Warrington and Widnes, to the east and south of Liverpool. Warrington Corporation started with an electric tramway in 1902, and this was finally closed in 1935. Motorbuses appeared from 1913. In 1970 the Warrington fleet of 70 buses comprised 64 double-deck and six single-deck, mainly Leylands and Daimlers with East Lancs bodies. The newest buses that year were 1970-delivered Bristol RESL6L with two-door Seddon bodies.

South-west of Warrington is nearby Widnes, which was unusual in this area as it never had trams, but started with motorbuses in 1909. Its 1970 fleet of 41 buses (32 double-deck, nine single-deck) was made up of Leylands with Leyland or East Lancs bodies. Its newest deliveries were two-door East Lancs-bodied Leyland Leopards delivered in 1969, and Widnes would go on to standardise on single-deckers.

In 1974 Widnes was transferred from Lancashire to Cheshire, as the new Halton district, and Halton was still running its own buses in 2007, as was Warrington.

The company bus operations on Merseyside were provided from the north by Ribble and from the south by Crosville. ∎

All three of the original undertakings that formed Merseyside PTE had bought Leyland Atlanteans, and this type would become the standard purchase until 1984. This is one of Liverpool's distinctive Metro-Cammell-bodied examples.
Edward Shirras

Liverpool chose Metro-Cammell-bodied Leyland Panthers to extend driver-only operation, but reverted to large batches of double-deckers when driver-only operation of these was legalised.
Edward Shirras

The last batch of buses to be delivered in Birkenhead livery went into service in November 1969, the month before the undertaking was absorbed into Merseyside PTE, and were Leyland Atlantean PDR1/2 with Northern Counties 71-seat bodies.
R L Wilson

Above: New in December 1970 to the PTE, but ordered by Birkenhead Corporation, were two of these rare single-deck Leyland Atlantean PDR2/1 with Northern Counties 40-seat bodies. One is seen at Woodside.
R L Wilson

Below: A famous bus – the former Wallasey Corporation no.1, one of the first four production Leyland Atlanteans, at Seacombe Ferry terminus in 1971, painted in PTE blue livery. It was new in 1958 with Metro-Cammell 77-seat body, and is now preserved.
R L Wilson

A reminder of the attractive Birkenhead Corporation livery, worn by a 1966 Leyland Titan PD2/40 with Massey 66-seat body, at the Woodside Ferry terminus. In PTE ownership, this bus was transferred across the Mersey to work with its brothers in the Liverpool division.
Geoff Lumb

Liverpool Corporation bought a large fleet of Leyland Panther PSUR1A/1 in 1968/69, with Metro-Cammell 47-seat two-door bodies.
Geoff Lumb

In a faded version of the distinctive Wallasey livery, shorn of references to that corporation other than the municipal crest, a 1960 Leyland Atlantean PDR1/1 with Metro-Cammell 76-seat body, at New Brighton in 1970.
Mark Page

Above: Two former Liverpool AEC Regent V D3RV lay over at Pier Head in 1970. They have Metro-Cammell 62-seat bodies, and the second bus is still in unpainted aluminium finish.
Mark Page

Below: The body design produced by Metro-Cammell for Liverpool's Leyland Atlanteans helped to convince other operators and bodybuilders that double-deckers need not be featureless boxes. This 1963 PDR1/1 77-seater was one of 380 similar buses delivered between 1962 and 1967.
Tony Wilson

St Helens Corporation ordered over 70 AEC Swifts between 1968 and 1975. This is one of the 1968 deliveries, an MP2R model with Marshall 44-seat body.
R L Wilson

Southport bought Leyland Panthers in 1968 and 1971. This is a 1968 PSUR1A/1R model with Metro-Cammell 45-seat body.
R L Wilson

The narrow streets of Warrington caused the corporation to specify 12 of these narrower (7ft 6in-wide) Leyland Titan PD2/40 Specials with East Lancs 64-seat forward entrance bodies in 1965.
Ian G Holt

Above: Delivered to Warrington late in 1970 were eight of these unusual Bristol RESL6L with Pennine 41-seat bodies.
P Hulin

Below: In recent years, Widnes and its successor, Halton, has favoured single-deckers, but a reminder of its double-deck fleet is provided by this 1959 Leyland Titan PD2/40 with East Lancs 63-seat body.

Above: In 1970, the attractively-liveried St Helens fleet was four years away from absorption into Merseyside PTE. This is a 1967 Leyland Titan PD2A/27 with 65-seat East Lancs body; from 1968 St Helens turned to large batches of AEC Swift single-deckers.
Mark Page

Left: From the 1969 batch, a St Helens AEC Swift 2MP2R with 44-seat Marshall two-door body. Its last Swifts would be delivered directly to the PTE in 1975.
Geoff Lumb

The attractive seaside town of Southport also had red/cream buses, and the transport undertaking would also disappear into the PTE in 1974. A reminder of sunny days in Southport is provided by this 1952 Leyland Titan PD2/12 with 61-seat Weymann body.
Geoff Lumb

When this 1970 Warrington Daimler Fleetline CRG6LX with East Lancs 72-seat body was photographed, Tesco was luring shoppers with double Green Shield stamps.
Geoff Lumb

The all-Leyland Widnes fleet in 1970 included seven of these Leopard PSU4/1R with East Lancs 42-seat two-door bodies, bought between 1967 and 1969.
Geoff Lumb

# West and North Yorkshire

West Yorkshire Road Car was an early customer for the Bristol VRT, and this 1969 York-West Yorkshire VRTSL6G is seen outside York railway station.
Edward Shirras

The largest and most populous section of Yorkshire in 1970 was the North Riding and the substantial part of the West Riding that in 1974 would become West Yorkshire Metropolitan County. In the north are the Yorkshire Dales and Moors, with the A1 trunk road and the East Coast Main Line running north-south between them. Although the northern part of the area is less densely populated, from Leeds and Harrogate south the area centred on Leeds and Bradford is intensely urban, including important towns like Dewsbury, Halifax, Huddersfield and Wakefield.

In 1970 a variety of bus operators served this area, some with the word 'Yorkshire' in their company names. In North Yorkshire there were two former Tilling Group National Bus Company fleets, United Automobile Services and West Yorkshire Road Car, and south of them was NBC's former BET Group Yorkshire Woollen District Traction and Hebble Motor Services companies, and the formerly independent West Riding Automobile company, now part of NBC.

United Auto's influence stretched all the way from the Scottish border down to the Ripon area, although it had once stretched down into East Anglia as well. The company is covered in the Scotland and North-East England volume in this series, but it still had a significant presence in Yorkshire, with garages in towns throughout the area and route networks serving towns like Northallerton, Richmond, Ripon, Scarborough, Thirsk and Whitby.

West Yorkshire took over where the United territory stopped, with a network of routes serving places like Bradford, Harrogate, Ilkley, Keighley, Leeds and Skipton. West Yorkshire Road Car was formed in 1928 from the Harrogate & District company, reflecting the expansion of the company's territory. It was a Tilling & BAT company, and the LMS and LNE railway companies acquired an interest in 1928. West Yorkshire became a Tilling Group company in the 1942 reorganisation. In the 1930s West Yorkshire took over responsibility for managing and operating the former municipal transport services in Keighley and York. The local buses carried Keighley-West Yorkshire and York-West Yorkshire names. The York buses were operated under a joint committee.

The 1970 West Yorkshire fleet of 459 buses comprised 175 double-deck, 213 single-deck and 51 coaches. The Keighley fleet was 41 double-deck and 11 single-deck, and the York fleet 65 double-deck and 15 single-deck. All were Bristol/ECW products. The newest bus deliveries in 1970 were RELL6G saloons and VRTSL6G double-deckers.

Although NBC's former Tilling Group companies controlled a large part of north-eastern England, former BET Group companies were more in evidence around the more

West Yorkshire built up a substantial fleet of some 200 Bristol RELL6G with ECW bus bodies. This 1966 example is a 53-seater with the distinctive early front-end styling.
Edward Shirras

heavily-populated areas, often as a consequence of BET's tramway operations.

Yorkshire Woollen was based in Dewsbury, with a network of bus routes stretching to Bradford, Halifax, Huddersfield, Leeds and Wakefield. The company's roots were in tramways in the heavy woollen district of Yorkshire, although it started running motorbuses in 1913 and had replaced the trams by 1934. Its 1970 fleet of 242 buses comprised 108 double-deckers, 84 single-deckers and 50 coaches. The chassis were fairly evenly divided between AECs and Leylands, with some newer Daimlers, and bodies reflected the BET Group's preferred suppliers. The newest deliveries were Alexander-bodied Daimler Fleetlines and Leyland Atlanteans bought in 1967.

Hebble was one of the BET Group's smaller companies, with just 93 vehicles in 1970 (27 double-deck, 27 single-deck, 39 coaches). The business was set up in 1924 and grew in the 1920s. In 1929 the LMS and LNE railway companies bought the company outright and some services were transferred to the new Halifax Joint Omnibus Committee. BET Group bought an interest in 1932 and the company became involved in trunk services in the Bradford, Halifax and Huddersfield areas.

The newest Hebble bus deliveries in 1970 were Alexander-bodied Leyland Leopards and Marshall-bodied AEC Reliances, new in 1969.

West Riding had an unusual background. It started as the Wakefield & District tramway operation in 1905, bought buses from 1922 which were operated by the subsidiary West Riding Automobile company, and that name was adopted for the main company from 1935, after the trams had been abandoned.

There had been negotiations to sell the company to the British Transport Commission in 1948, but these fell through, so West Riding increased its territorial influence with the purchase of the J Bullock business in 1950, which brought with it 150 buses, virtually doubling the West Riding fleet.

West Riding was involved in the development of the notorious Guy Wulfrunian double-decker, which proved unreliable in service, and it also made other unfortunate vehicle choices, which helped to undermine its profitability. It sold out to the Transport Holding Company in 1967, passing into National Bus Company control from 1969.

Its 1970 fleet of 406 buses and coaches comprised 275 double-deckers, 104 single-deckers and 27 coaches, and the mix of vehicle types reflected its own vehicle policy plus the buses drafted in from fellow NBC companies to keep the route network around Wakefield, Pontefract and Leeds going. West Riding's newest single-deck buses had been AEC Swifts and Leyland Panthers bought in 1967, but from 1969 a large fleet of Bristol RELL6G with Plaxton and ECW bodies was delivered. Roe-bodied Daimler Fleetline double-deckers had also been bought in 1968/69 and Alexander- and Northern Counties-bodied Fleetlines would be bought to upgrade the fleet.

With several companies operating in a compact area of Yorkshire, it was inevitable that National Bus Company would look to rationalise its activities. It subsequently formed the West Riding group of companies, taking in Hebble, West Riding and Yorkshire Woollen, but Hebble quickly became a coaching company, with its buses redistributed among its sister companies, and then became the nucleus of National Travel (North East). West Riding and Yorkshire Woollen were sold in 1987 to its management team, and as Caldaire Holdings the business was sold on to British Bus in 1995; the operations are now part of the Arriva empire.

Left: In an area where former BET Group fleets were dominant, West Yorkshire was the main bastion of Tilling practice. At Keighley bus station, wearing Keighley-West Yorkshire fleetnames, a 1963 Bristol FS6B Lodekka with ECW 60-seat body. Behind is a recently-delivered Bristol VRT.
Geoff Lumb

Below: The York-West Yorkshire fleet also included examples of Bristol's lightweight LH model. This is a 1970 LH6L with 45-seat ECW body.
Geoff Lumb

West Yorkshire Road Car was sold in 1987 to a senior management partnership, but was reorganised over the following years, selling the West Yorkshire and York businesses to Yorkshire Rider, and retaining the Harrogate & District, Keighley & District and Yorkshire Coastliner companies, which passed to Blazefield in 1991, and are now part of Transdev.

Yorkshire still boasted some substantial municipal fleets in 1970, at Bradford, Halifax, Huddersfield, Leeds and Todmorden.

Bradford had company-operated horse trams and steam trams from 1882, and the corporation started running electric trams in 1898, taking over the company tramways in 1902. The trams had been replaced by 1950, but in 1911 it vied with nearby Leeds to operate the UK's first trolleybus system. This grew dramatically and was the UK's last system, closing in 1972. Motorbuses were introduced in 1926.

The 1970 Bradford City Transport motorbus fleet comprised 281 vehicles (269 double-deck, 12 single-deck) and there were still 81 double-deck trolleybuses. The motorbuses were AECs, Daimlers and Leylands with bodies by a range of builders. The trolleybuses were BUTs, Karriers and Sunbeams, rebodied by East Lancs, some with forward-entrance bodies. Bradford had

bought its last new trolleybus in 1950 but continued to stock its fleet with vehicles withdrawn when other systems closed.

The newest motorbuses in 1970 were Alexander-bodied two-door Daimler Fleetlines, supplied in that year. It would go on to buy Alexander-bodied Leyland Atlanteans.

Halifax had electric trams from 1898 to 1939, dabbled briefly in trolleybus operation between 1921 and 1926, and bought its first motorbuses in 1912, though it was another decade before serious purchases were made. A Halifax Joint Committee was set up between the corporation and the LMS and LNE railway companies in 1929, and A, B and C fleets were established: the A fleet was run within the Halifax boundaries by the corporation; the B fleet was run by the corporation for the Joint Committee and worked outer suburban routes; the C fleet were longer routes operated by the railway companies. As we have seen, the railway companies bought the Hebble business in 1930, and this resulted in buses working B services transferring to the joint committee and those for C services operated by railway-owned Hebble.

In 1970 there were 186 buses in the Halifax fleet (124 double-deckers, 53 single-deckers, nine coaches), of AEC, Daimler, Dennis and Leyland make. The newest deliveries had been Northern Counties-bodied Daimler Fleetlines and Pennine-bodied Fleetline single-deckers.

Huddersfield was another town where the buses were run by the corporation and a joint committee. Unusually, the corporation was given powers to operate its own tramway, which opened with steam trams in 1883. Electric trams followed in 1901, and had been replaced by trolleybuses by 1940. Trolleybuses were first introduced in 1933 and motorbuses in 1920.

The LMS railway bought half of the Huddersfield motorbus undertaking in 1930, creating the joint committee; the corporation fleet used only trolleybuses from 1930 to 1950, when the first corporation motorbuses were bought. The corporation and joint committee fleets were distinguished by the application of the red/cream livery: the corporation buses had a cream streamlined effect at the front.

Later West Yorkshire Bristol RELL6Gs had the deep flat screens; this is a 1970 example with 53-seat ECW body. Geoff Lumb

Huddersfield had replaced its last trolleybuses with motorbuses in 1968 and the 1970 fleet totalled 221 buses, 180 double-deckers and 41 single-deckers, mainly AECs and Daimlers with bodywork by East Lancs and Roe. The latest deliveries at the time were corporation Seddon RUs with Pennine bodies, and Roe-bodied Fleetlines for both the corporation and joint committee fleets.

In 1969 Huddersfield Corporation had bought the stage services of the long-established Hansons Buses Ltd, and the remaining coach business would pass to West Yorkshire PTE in 1974. A number of Hanson buses passed into the Huddersfield fleet, and some survived to join the PTE fleet.

Leeds City Transport was by far the largest municipal operation in West Yorkshire, with 715 buses in 1970 (601 double-deck, 114 single-deck). Leeds believed in multi-sourcing its chassis, so there were AECs, Daimlers and Leylands, though over 70 per cent of the bodywork was built locally, by Roe, and the rest by Metro-Cammell and Park Royal.

Leeds Corporation leased track to a horse tram company in 1871, and these were followed by steam trams in 1879. The corporation assumed control in 1894, and electric trams started running in 1897. The substantial tramway system closed in 1959. Leeds also experimented with trolleybuses, introducing them on the same day in 1911 as Bradford, but the small Leeds system was closed in 1928. Motorbuses appeared in 1906, but only really became established in the 1920s.

The newest buses in the Leeds City Transport fleet, delivered in 1970, were two-door Roe-bodied Daimler Fleetlines and Leyland Atlanteans from substantial batches, as well as two-door single-deck Park Royal-bodied Fleetlines and six Mercedes-Benz L405D, bought for a city centre service, an early use of minibuses in an urban setting.

The other municipal operation in 1970 was at Todmorden, a Pennine town on the Lancashire/Yorkshire border that actually had a Lancashire address in 1970, but which had greater links with Yorkshire.

Todmorden Corporation started running motorbuses in 1907 to compete with company-owned horsebuses and in 1931 a joint committee was set up following the sale of half of the undertaking to the LMS railway. Roughly half of the fleet was owned by the corporation and the other half by the railway interests. In 1970 the Todmorden Joint Omnibus Committee had 27 buses (10 double-deck, 17 single-deck), all Leylands, as the fleet had been for half a century.

The interests of the British Railways Board in the joint undertakings at Halifax, Huddersfield and Todmorden, as at Sheffield, had been transferred on 1 January 1969 to Amalgamated Passenger Transport, a wholly-owned subsidiary of the newly-operational National Bus Company.

There would be further changes involving Halifax and Todmorden in 1971, when the joint fleets in these towns, together with the local services of Hebble, were placed under a new Calderdale Joint Omnibus Committee. This committee had only a short existence, because in 1974 West Yorkshire Metropolitan County was created and the West Yorkshire PTE absorbed the Bradford, Calderdale, Halifax, Huddersfield and Leeds bus operations. The PTE bus operations, by that time Yorkshire Rider, were sold to a management-led employee buy-out in 1988, and were sold on to Badgerline in 1994, now part of First.

With network coverage by big territorial companies there were fewer well-known independents in north and west Yorkshire.

Two businesses in the Mirfield area were J J Longstaff (six vehicles in 1970) and Joseph Wood & Son (five vehicles), operating jointly between Dewsbury and Mirfield. In the York area were Reliance, Sutton-on-the-Forest, operating Easingwold-York, and York Pullman, operating to Easingwold, Linton, Stamford Bridge and Holme-upon-Spalding Moor. In 1970 the York Pullman fleet had recently received Roe- and Plaxton-bodied AEC Swifts and would go on to buy what had become a staple for Yorkshire independents, Roe-bodied Daimler Fleetlines.

Probably the best-known independent in the West Riding was Pennine Motor Services of Gargrave, a firm that started in 1925 and survived into 2007. The main routes link Gargrave with Settle, Skipton and Burnley. The newest vehicles in its 13-strong all-Leyland fleet in 1970 were Willowbrook dual-purpose-bodied Leyland Leopards bought in 1969.

Also based in the West Riding was Britain's largest coach company, Wallace Arnold Tours Ltd, with a fleet of over 300 vehicles, mostly coaches. The buses were for its subsidiary bus-operating companies, Hardwicks Services of Scarborough, acquired in 1952. Other bus-operating subsidiaries, Farsley Omnibus and Kippax & District, had been sold to Leeds City Transport in 1968. ∎

Above: Following the early deliveries of Bristol VRTSL6Gs in 1969, West Yorkshire went on to buy a substantial fleet of this NBC standard model.
Mark Page

Opposite top: Yorkshire Woollen bought AECs and Leylands in fairly equal quantities. This is a 1961 AEC Regent V 2D3RA with Northern Counties 70-seat forward entrance body, in Leeds in 1970.
Mark Page

Right: Unusual secondhand acquisitions for a former BET Group company were the Bristol Ks transferred to Yorkshire Woollen from West Yorkshire Road Car. This is a 1955 K5G with 55-seat ECW highbridge body.
Ted Jones

Far right: Other transfers into the Yorkshire Woollen fleet were buses from the former Sheffield Joint Omnibus Committee, following its break-up in 1970. This is an ex-Sheffield JOC 1962 Leyland Atlantean with 78-seat Weymann body, passing the Edinburgh Corporation-style former Leyland demonstration Titan PD2/20 with Metro-Cammell Orion 63-seat body. Unused to the luxury of three destination boxes, YWD seems to have decided to use the upper display for the company name, though passengers might be confused into thinking that Yorkshire is the ultimate destination.
Ted Jones

Right: An uncompromising view of
1960s Yorkshire, with cobbled streets,
dark stone buildings and, as this is
Bradford, trolleybus overhead. The
bus is a 1960 Hebble AEC Regent V
with 71-seat forward entrance
Metro-Cammell bodywork.
Geoff Lumb

Below: The small Hebble fleet also
included single-deck buses. This is a
1959 AEC Reliance 2MU3RV with
BET-style Willowbrook 43-seat body.
Geoff Lumb

Below: The ambitious but ultimately
flawed Guy Wulfrunian did little for
Guy or for its sponsor, West Riding.
By 1970 the Wulfrunian population
was already reducing, but this 1963
example was still in service in 1970,
as seen at Wakefield bus station.
The Wulfrunians had all gone by 1972,
some after barely seven years service.
Mark Page

Above: Under state control, new and secondhand buses were quickly drafted in to update the West Riding fleet. This is a 1970 Bristol RELL6G with 53-seat ECW body, one of 39 bought in 1970-72.

Royston Morgan

Below: Nearly 100 Daimler Fleetlines joined the West Riding fleet between 1967 and 1972. This is one of 55 CRG6LX with 76-seat Roe bodies delivered in 1968/69. Behind is a Guy Arab IV/Roe lowbridge, and behind that a United Services ex-Ribble Leyland Titan PD1/3 with Burlingham body.

Mark Page

Left: The only surviving trolleybus system left in Britain after 1970 was Bradford, which survived Walsall by two years and closed in 1972. The final fleet consisted mostly of rebodied chassis from the Bradford fleet and from other systems that had closed. This bus, seen in 1970, started life as a Sunbeam F4 single-decker with the BET-owned Mexborough & Swinton system in 1950, was bought by Bradford in 1963 and received this forward entrance East Lancs 66-seat body the same year.
Omnicolour/Martin Llewellyn

Below: The Bradford motorbus fleet in 1970 was a mix of AECs, Daimlers and Leylands. This is a 1963 AEC Regent V 2D3RA with 70-seat forward entrance Metro-Cammell body, one of 120 similar buses bought between 1959 and 1964.
Tony Wilson

Bradford stuck to front-engined double-deckers until it bought Atlanteans and Fleetlines in 1967. This is a 1967 Leyland Titan PD3A/2 with East Lancs 70-seat forward entrance body; Bradford would buy more PD3A/2s in 1969. *Geoff Lumb*

A 1968 Bradford Leyland Atlantean PDR1/3 with Metro-Cammell 74-seat body. *Geoff Lumb*

The Halifax fleet invariably included some unusual buses, and in 1967 five of these Dennis Loline III with Northern Counties 74-seat forward entrance bodies were bought – at a time when Dennis chassis were still fairly rare. In 1970 they were sold to West Riding. *Geoff Lumb*

Halifax bought the single-deck version of the Daimler Fleetline, the SRG6LX, with Willowbrook and Pennine bodies in 1967/69. This is a rather battered 1967 Willowbrook-bodied 45-seater.
Geoff Lumb

Unusual buses in the Halifax fleet were short-tailed AEC Reliance 6MU3RA with 39-seat Pennine bodies, bought in 1966.
Geoff Lumb

In the 1960s the Huddersfield Corporation and Joint Omnibus Committee fleets had taken batches of Roe-bodied forward entrance Daimler CVG6LX and this 1964 65-seater was new to the JOC fleet. It would pass with the Huddersfield fleet to West Yorkshire PTE in 1974.
Mark Page

Above: In 1970 Huddersfield took delivery of the first of 23 Seddon RU, 17 of them with Pennine 45-seat bodies like this bus seen at Fernside late in 1970.
Omnicolour/Martin Llewellyn

Left: The Hanson bus business had passed to Huddersfield Corporation late in 1969. The Hanson fleet was notable for rebuilt and rebodied AECs: this 1955 AEC Reliance started life with a Plaxton coach body but later received this Roe 41-seat bus body, and a new registration. It passed into the Huddersfield fleet.
Geoff Lumb

Left: The traditional face of Leeds buses – a 1951 AEC Regent III with Roe 56-seat body featuring deep windows and the famous pear-shaped staircase window.
Geoff Lumb

Below: Still in the Leeds fleet in 1970, a 1950 AEC Regent III/Roe, laying over at Leeds central bus station.
Mark Page

Between 1966 and 1971 Leeds bought 120 AEC Swift with 48-seat two-door bodies by Metro-Cammell, Park Royal and Roe. This is a 1967 MP2R model with Metro-Cammell body.
Geoff Lumb

Bought for the 72 Leeds-Bradford route, this 1962 Daimler CVG6LX/30, seen in Bradford, has 70-seat Roe forward entrance bodywork.
Geoff Lumb

Comparing with the Roe-bodied Daimler, an unusual 30ft-long AEC Regent V with exposed radiator and Metro-Cammell Orion 70-seat body, one of 14 bought in 1960.
Geoff Lumb

Above: For its driver-only buses, Leeds adopted this livery using two shades of green, worn here by a 1964 Daimler Fleetline CRG6LX with 70-seat Roe body.
Royston Morgan

Below: In Bradford in 1970, a new Leeds Leyland Atlantean PDR2/1 with 78-seat Roe body, one of 240 long Atlanteans bought between 1968 and 1974.
Tony Wilson

Todmorden JOC was a staunch Leyland user right to the end of its existence, and this 1951 all-Leyland Titan PD2/12 sits under the railway arches at the main Todmorden bus terminal. It carries the simplified coat-of-arms showing just the Todmorden crest.
Geoff Lumb

A well-loaded Todmorden 1950 all-Leyland Titan PD2/1 illustrates the cramped upper deck on the lowbridge body layout. The coat-of-arms on the side combines the Todmorden Corporation crest with British Railways lettering where previously the LMS railway's badge was shown.
Geoff Lumb

The last buses delivered to Todmorden JOC before the creation of Calderdale JOC in 1971 were six Leyland Leopard PSU4/2R with Pennine 45-seat bodies.
Geoff Lumb

A notable vehicle in the fleet of Wood, based in Mirfield, to the north-east of Huddersfield, was this 1964 Leyland Atlantean PDR1/1 with Park Royal body, a former Leyland demonstrator. It is seen in Dewsbury.
Mark Page

York Pullman was another well-known independent operator in the Yorkshire area. This is a 1957 AEC Regent V MD3RV with 61-seat Roe body.
Geoff Lumb

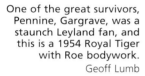

One of the great survivors, Pennine, Gargrave, was a staunch Leyland fan, and this is a 1954 Royal Tiger with Roe bodywork.
Geoff Lumb

A later Pennine Leyland, a 1970 Leopard PSU3A/4R with Willowbrook 49-seat dual-purpose body.
Geoff Lumb

# South and East Yorkshire

Castlegate, Sheffield with three Sheffield buses. On the right is a 1963 AEC Regent V with Park Royal 70-seat forward entrance body from the Corporation/British Railways jointly-owned B fleet, and behind are two 1959 Leyland Titan PD3/1 with Roe 69-seat bodies, from the corporation-owned A fleet.
*Mark Page*

Yorkshire and the Humber is England's largest region, covering an area of just under 6,000 sq ml with a population of around five million. It has boundaries with County Durham, Lincolnshire, Nottinghamshire, Derbyshire, Lancashire, Westmorland and the North Sea. In 1970 it was divided into Ridings, and in this section we are looking at the East Riding, and that part of the West Riding that is now South Yorkshire County. Although the name Humberside was used from 1974 for a trans-Humber county that embraced the East Riding and parts of North Lincolnshire, in 1996 the East Riding name was restored for one of two new unitary authorities north of the Humber, the other being Kingston-upon-Hull.

South Yorkshire, to use the post-1974 name, covers the area centred on four main towns – Barnsley, Doncaster, Rotherham and the city of Sheffield. The economy was built on steel and coal-mining and, around Doncaster, railways. In 1970 these industries were still important to the local economy, and there was a dense network of local bus services.

Like so many other places, Sheffield had company-operated horse trams, from 1873, and the corporation acquired the system in 1896, with electric traction following three years later. Motorbuses started in 1913, and the well-regarded tramway system was closed in 1960, although some cars were barely eight years old.

Like some of the other Yorkshire municipalities, Sheffield became involved in operating services on behalf of the mainline railway companies. In 1929 the corporation took over management of the longer-distance bus services operated by the LMS and LNE railway companies, under the Sheffield Joint Omnibus Committee. The bus fleet was then subdivided into the corporation-owned A fleet, the B fleet that was jointly owned by the corporation and the railway companies, and the C fleet that was totally railway-owned. This situation continued into British Railways days.

The A, B and C fleets tended to have different types of bus, though there tended to be more similarities between B and C fleet buses, which included more single-deckers, as well as double-deckers with rear platform doors and unique batches of ECW-bodied Leyland Leopards and Titans, a consequence of the railway involvement.

The 1970 Sheffield fleet consisted of 724 buses (661 double-deck, 63 single-deck), dominated by Leylands and AECs, with a growing fleet of Daimlers. Most favoured bodybuilders were Metro-Cammell, Roe and Park Royal.

The newest vehicles in 1970 were Park Royal-bodied AEC Swifts and Leyland Atlanteans, and Alexander-bodied Leyland Leopard coaches, delivered new that year.

In 1969 the British Railways Board interests in the joint committees at Halifax, Huddersfield, Sheffield and Todmorden had been transferred to a wholly-owned NBC subsidiary, Amalgamated Passenger Transport Ltd. And on 1 January 1970 the Sheffield Joint Committee was dissolved, with some routes and vehicles passing to National Bus Company control.

The other municipal operations in what would become South Yorkshire were at Doncaster and Rotherham.

Doncaster was served by horsebuses from the 1880s but the corporation opened an electric tramway system in 1902, but trolleybuses were introduced from 1928 and the trams lasted until 1935. Motorbuses had been used from 1922, and finally replaced the trolleybuses in 1963.

The bus fleet at the beginning of 1970 consisted of 110 vehicles (78 double-deck, 32 single-deck), a mix of AECs, Daimlers and Leylands, all with Roe bodies. Doncaster Corporation's newest buses delivered during 1970 were Seddon RUs with Pennine two-door bodies and Daimler Fleetlines with two-door Roe bodies.

Rotherham had electric trams from 1903, then trolleybuses from 1912. The last tram route, to Sheffield, survived until 1949, and the

1970 deliveries to Sheffield included the last of 160 long wheelbase Leyland Atlantean PDR2/1 with Park Royal 79-seat bodies bought since 1968.
Omnicolour/Chris Aston

trolleybus system closed in 1965. Motorbuses appeared in 1913. In 1970 Rotherham had 127 buses (113 double-deck, 14 single-deck), dominated by Daimler chassis and Roe bodies. The newest deliveries in 1970 were two-door Roe-bodied Daimler Fleetlines.

NBC's main presence in South Yorkshire was the Yorkshire Traction company, descended from the tram-operating Barnsley & District company, which had also started operating motorbuses. The Yorkshire Traction name was adopted in 1928 and the company grew by acquisition in the 1930s. Following the formation of National Bus Company in 1969, a tidying-up exercise placed two smaller subsidiaries under Yorkshire Traction control. These were Mexborough & Swinton and County Motors.

Mexborough & Swinton had operated electric trams (1907-29) and trolleybuses (1915-61), and motorbuses from 1922. County Motors had been owned by the two BET fleets, Yorkshire Traction and Yorkshire Woollen, as well as the formerly independent West Riding company. After West Riding passed into state ownership at the end of 1967 County was amalgamated into Yorkshire Traction.

Yorkshire Traction's service network was based on Barnsley, with regular departures to main towns like Doncaster, Huddersfield and Rotherham.

Sheffield's big Leyland Atlantean PDR2/1 with 79-seat Park Royal bodies were undoubtedly impressive buses in the white/dark blue livery. This newly-delivered example is seen in 1970.
M A Penn

The Yorkshire Traction fleet in 1970 contained 400 buses and coaches (199 double-deck, 162 single-deck, 39 coaches), mostly Leylands with a wide variety of bodies.

South Yorkshire was an area with a good selection of independent bus operators, notably round the Doncaster area. Here, famously, a number of operators worked services from surrounding towns and villages into the centre of Doncaster, often jointly with each other and with company and municipal operators.

In 1970 there were still seven small independent operators working into Doncaster, and all had started up in the 1920s. Although their names were well-known to enthusiasts and locals, they all had small fleets that were a mix of service buses, mostly double-deckers, and coaches for private hire and local tour work. Most were based in smaller communities in an arc radiating to the east of Doncaster. On services from, variously, Goole, Thorne, Stainforth and Armthorpe to the north-east were Blue Line and its associated company, Reliance; Felix; Premier; and Severn. From Rossington in the south-east ran the buses of Blue Ensign, and Rossie, while Leon worked in from Finningley.

Blue Line was Samuel Morgan Ltd of Armthorpe, and the associated Reliance company was R Store of Stainforth. The joint fleet totalled 25 vehicles (12 double-deckers, 13 coaches) and Guy Arabs had been favoured for many years. The newest bus delivery, in 1967, was a forward-entrance Roe-bodied Arab V. Felix Motors of Hatfield had favoured AECs, but in 1970 its most recent bus was a 1969 Roe-bodied Daimler Fleetline. Its fleet consisted of nine double-deckers and six coaches. Premier was Harold Wilson Ltd, Stainforth, with a 1970 fleet of 22 (five double-deck, one single-deck, 16 coaches); its newest purchase

in 1970 was a 1965 Fleetline/Roe. T Severn & Sons of Dunscroft had 14 vehicles (nine double-deck, one single-deck, four coaches) and was a Leyland fan; its newest delivery was a 1969 Roe-bodied Atlantean.

Blue Ensign, G H Ennifer Ltd, was actually based in Doncaster. In 1970 it had just six vehicles, three double-deckers and three coaches, the newest bus being a 1967 Fleetline/Roe. Rossie Motors, Rossington, had a fleet of nine vehicles, five double-deckers and four coaches, the newest bus being a 1964 Daimler CVG6.30/Roe.

Leon Motor Services of Finningley had a relatively large fleet – 28 vehicles, comprising 10 double-deckers, four single-deckers and 14 coaches.

After 1970 the Doncaster independents all took advantage of the Bus Grants scheme to buy new double-deckers, and five of them chose very similar Roe-bodied Fleetlines; Severn chose Roe-bodied Atlanteans, while Premier went for Alexander-bodied buses, an Atlantean and a Volvo Ailsa.

As it turned out the Doncaster independents had less than a decade to go, as the new South Yorkshire PTE set about buying up independents throughout its area, and all but Leon and Premier were acquired by the PTE by 1980.

The Doncaster, Rotherham and Sheffield municipal undertakings were all absorbed by the South Yorkshire PTE

Sheffield A fleet received 20 of these Leyland Atlantean PDR1/2 with 77-seat Neepsend-built East Lancs bodies in 1966.
T K Brookes

when it was created in 1974. Yorkshire Traction was sold to its management team in 1987 and remained out of the grasp of the major groups until 2005, when the business was sold to Stagecoach.

In 1970 the East Riding of Yorkshire was dominated by two bus operators – NBC's East Yorkshire, and Kingston-upon-Hull Corporation.

East Yorkshire was formed by merging local operators and in 1929 the LNE railway took a shareholding. As a BAT group company it passed into BET Group control in 1942. It covered a substantial area, bounded by the North Sea on the east and the River Humber to the south, that stretched inland to Selby, Goole, York and Malton, and north to Bridlington and Scarborough.

The East Yorkshire fleet in 1970 consisted of 236 buses and coaches (132 double-deck, 53 single-deck, 21 coaches and 30 semi-coaches). For years many of East Yorkshire's double-deckers had an inward-sloping upper deck contour to pass through the Gothic arch of the Beverley Bar. The 1970 fleet was evenly divided between AECs and Leylands, with some more recent Daimlers, and bodywork was the usual BET mix. The newest deliveries, in 1969, were Park Royal-bodied Fleetlines and Marshall-bodied Leyland Leopards.

The one municipal operation in East Yorkshire in 1970 was Kingston-upon-Hull Corporation. The city had horse trams, steam trams and, from 1899, electric trams. The tramway system was replaced by trolleybuses from 1937 and the last tram ran in 1945; the last trolleybus ran in 1964.

Motorbuses were tried briefly in Hull in 1909 and, on a continuous basis, from 1921. The 1970 bus fleet consisted of 239 vehicles (210 double-deck, 29 single-deck) of AEC and Leyland manufacture, with Park Royal, Roe and Weymann bodies. The newest buses in 1970 were Roe-bodied Leyland Atlanteans delivered that year; Hull built up a substantial fleet of Roe Atlanteans between 1961 and 1975.

In preparation for the privatisation of the National Bus Company, the giant United Automobile company territory was split, and East Yorkshire gained services around the Scarborough area. East Yorkshire was sold to its management team in 1987. Twenty years later it was still a privately-owned business, still beyond the grasp of the big groups.

What had become Kingston-upon-Hull City Transport was sold in 1993 to a consortium formed by Cleveland Transit, already in private hands, and KHCT employees – but a year later Cleveland Transit sold to Stagecoach, and with it went the Hull operation.

Based in Pontefract was South Yorkshire Motors, which started as part of the Bullock family's empire, running services in the Leeds, Pontefract, Doncaster, Barnsley and Selby areas. Its 1970 fleet of 17 buses included Leyland Titans and Atlanteans, the newest bought in 1967. Although the considerably larger South Yorkshire PTE would in 1974 adopt a similar name, South Yorkshire Motors changed its name to South Yorkshire Road Transport.

Also Pontefract-based was United Services, a partnership of operators, which by 1970 was down to just two – W R & P Bingley and Cooper Bros. The company operated between Wakefield, Doncaster and Hemsworth. The combined Bingley and Cooper fleets in 1970 operated five double-deckers, 25 coaches and a minibus, with the Bingley fleet considerably larger. Leyland Leopards with Plaxton dual-purpose bodies were the newest purchases, bought in 1969/70. Bingley would acquire Cooper in 1977, and then sold the business on to West Yorkshire PTE the same year. ∎

Laying over in Sheffield, two 1960 Sheffield AEC Regent V 2D3RA. The B fleet bus on the right has Roe 69-seat bodywork, complete with platform doors, and the bus on the left, from the A fleet, has 69-seat Weymann Orion body.
Geoff Lumb

An unusual combination bought for the Sheffield A fleet in 1959 was the AEC Regent V 2D3RA with Alexander 69-seat bodywork.
Geoff Lumb

Sheffield buses escaped the industrial landscape into the Peak District, like this 1957 Leyland Titan PD2/20 with Roe 59-seat body.
Geoff Lumb

This Doncaster Corporation Roe-bodied Daimler CVG6 is not quite what it seems. The body was built in the late-1950s, fitted to a secondhand trolleybus, and following the abandonment of the trolleybus system, which was completed in 1963, 20 such bodies were remounted on motorbus chassis. This chassis was new in 1962 and the wider pillar on the upper deck provides a clue to the body's ancestry. Geoff Lumb

Leaving Doncaster's South bus station, a Doncaster Corporation 1963 Leyland Titan PD3/4 with 70-seat Roe forward entrance body. On the left is a Daimler CD650/30 with Roe bodywork from the fleet of Leon, Finningley. Mark Page

Unusual purchases by a Yorkshire municipality were AEC/Park Royal Renowns, bought by Rotherham Corporation in 1964, following experience with a batch of AEC/Park Royal Bridgemasters. Geoff Lumb

Doncaster bought 10 rare Leyland Royal Tiger Cub RTC1/2 in 1969, fitted with Roe 45-seat bodies. The Royal Tiger Cub was primarily an export model, a longer and more powerful Tiger Cub, and Doncaster took the only home market examples, 10 in 1965 and 10 in 1969.
Edward Shirras

In 1970/72 Doncaster went for the new Seddon RU and the 14 1970-delivered models had Seddon's own Pennine 42-seat body, like the bus seen leaving Doncaster's Northern bus station.
M Fowler

In 1970 Doncaster also received eight Daimler Fleetline CRG6LX with 74-seat Roe bodies.
M A Penn

Above: Rotherham bought its first rear-engined double-deckers in 1968, Daimler Fleetline CRG6LX with 78-seat Roe bodies.
A C Turner-Bishop

Below: The first Daimlers in the Leyland-dominated Yorkshire Traction fleet were seven Fleetline CRG6LXB with Alexander-influenced Roe 75-seat bodies bought in 1968. More Fleetlines would follow in 1969-71, including the single-deck version.
B D Nicholson

Built and painted for Devon General, four Willowbrook 75-seat Leyland Atlantean PDR1A/1 were diverted to Yorkshire Traction in 1969.
Royston Morgan

Barnsley bus station was the hub of Yorkshire Traction's activities, and here is a 1961 Leyland Titan PD3A/1 with Northern Counties 73-seat bodywork passing, on the left, a 1958 Park Royal-bodied Leyland Tiger Cub.
Geoff Lumb

The Blue Ensign fleet was always smartly presented, right down to the lined-out livery and chrome wheeltrims. This is a 1967 Daimler Fleetline CRG6LX with 78-seat body leaving Doncaster South bus station.
Royston Morgan

Samuel Morgan Ltd's Blue Line fleet favoured Guy Arabs, and this is a 1967 Arab V with 73-seat forward entrance body, at the famous Doncaster Christchurch terminus.
Geoff Lumb

Left: Felix, Hatfield, bought AEC Regent V with Roe 73-seat bodies, like this 1963 example.
Geoff Lumb

Below: The distinctive blue of Leon, Finningley, on its 1958 Daimler CD650/30 with 73-seat Roe body, looks out from the dark recesses of Doncaster's South bus station.
Mark Page

Left: **Premier, Stainforth, bought this 78-seat Roe-bodied Daimler Fleetline CRG6LX in 1965.**
R I Stacey

Below: **Similar to a batch built for Leeds, this Daimler CVD6/30 with Roe 73-seat body was delivered to Rossie, Rossington, in 1962.**
K W Swallow

Above: **Right at the start of 1971, Severn, Dunscroft, received these two Leyland Atlantean PDR1A/1 with 75-seat Alexander bodies.**
M Fowler

Below: **South Yorkshire Motors received two of these Roe 70-seat Leyland Atlantean PDR1/2 in 1967, as seen at Pontefract bus station.**
A C Nightingale

Harold Wilson's Premier fleet was fairly mixed and included this 1959 Guy Arab IV with 65-seat Roe body bought new, like most of the buses owned by the Doncaster area independents.
Mark Page

Rossie, Rossington, was a long-term Daimler fan, and this is a 1964 CVG6/30 with the inevitable Roe 73-seat forward entrance body.
Geoff Lumb

Severn, Dunscroft, favoured Leylands. This is a one of two Titan PD3/4 with Roe 72-seat bodies bought in 1961; further examples were bought in 1963/64.
Geoff Lumb

In the distinctive dark blue/cream livery of East Yorkshire, a 1955 Leyland Titan PD2/12 with 56-seat Roe lowbridge body, outside Hull Paragon railway station.
Geoff Lumb

A distinctive feature on many East Yorkshire double-deckers was the modified roof contour to allow them to pass through the Gothic arch of Beverley Bar. This is very obvious on this 1956 AEC Regent V MD3RV with 56-seat Willowbrook body.
Omnicolour/Martin Llewellyn

The modified roof contour on some East Yorkshire double-deckers continued in simplified form with deliveries of newer types, like this 1966 AEC Renown 3B3RA with Park Royal 68-seat body.
Geoff Lumb

An East Yorkshire AEC Renown 3B3RA with Park Royal 70-seat body, one of 14 delivered in 1965.
Edward Shirras

An East Yorkshire Leyland Tiger Cub PSUC1/2 with 41-seat dual-purpose Metro-Cammell body, one of eight delivered in 1960.
Edward Shirras

East Yorkshire's dual-purpose vehicles found themselves in many parts of eastern England. This 1964 Leyland Leopard PSU3/3R with 47-seat Willowbrook body, is at Newcastle.
Edward Shirras

Above:
Photographed in Hull in 1969, a former Nottingham AEC Regent III/Park Royal 56-seater, one of a number acquired by Kingston-upon-Hull.
Edward Shirras

Left: In 1964-66 Kingston-upon-Hull bought 12 Leyland Panther PSUR1/1 with Roe bodies; this is a 1965 45-seater.
Edward Shirras

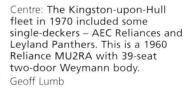

Above: Photographed in Leeds in 1970, an East Yorkshire 1968 Leyland Panther Cub PSRC1/1 with Marshall 45-seat bus body.
Mark Page

Centre: The Kingston-upon-Hull fleet in 1970 included some single-deckers – AEC Reliances and Leyland Panthers. This is a 1960 Reliance MU2RA with 39-seat two-door Weymann body.
Geoff Lumb

Left: Kingston-upon-Hull built up a fleet of over 100 Roe-bodied Leyland Atlantean PDR1/1 in the 1960s; this is a 1968 75-seat example, still in the corporation's distinctive streamline livery. Note the unusual one-piece flat driver's windscreen.
Geoff Lumb